Fighting fit: a memoir **Chanie Rosenberg**

Fighting fit: a memoir Chanie Rosenberg

REDWORDS

Fighting fit: A memoir by Chanie Rosenberg
Published by Redwords June 2013

ISBN: 978 1 909026 31 5

Design and production: Roger Huddle

Printed by The Russell Press

Redwords is linked to Bookmarks: the
socialist bookshop

1 Bloomsbury Street London WC1B 3QE

redwords.org.uk

bookmarksbookshop.co.uk

6

The Socialist Workers Party (SWP), that I've spent most of my years building, has been well served in terms of its history. My husband, Tony Cliff, published an autobiography called *A World to Win*, which discusses the political background of the SWP. Ian Birchall has covered his life in an excellent biography, which is a meticulous analysis of the theory and practice of the SWP from its roots to the year 2000. So is there a need for something more?

My hope is to show that we revolutionaries are people like anyone else. We have social and cultural aspects to our lives which are part and parcel of our struggle for a different world. What happens between the evening meeting and the weekend paper sale? What about family life? And why do people become revolutionaries in the first place? We do not want a revolution in order to have yet more meetings and get cold and wet on street corners forever. Under capitalism it is virtually impossible to live the full life that Marx talked about for the future – to 'hunt in the morning, fish in the afternoon, rear cattle in the evening, criticise after dinner'; but that is what we are fighting for, and what sustains us in swimming against the tide. So this is my humble contribution to understanding a revolutionary life in the round.

Introduction

I want to thank Donny Gluckstein for his help tidying up the draft, Ewa Widowson for her careful perusal of the draft and important and useful suggestions, and the staff of Hackney Library and Exchange Group Training Centres, who were extremely friendly and helpful on the technical side of writing this booklet, Kamila Balcewicz, Edyta Blas and Ania Mikolajczyk.

8

Part 1
South Africa

I was born in Cape Town, South Africa, in April 1922. At that time it was a thoroughly racist society in which the whites had everything and the blacks virtually nothing. The government did not even count the latters' numbers. Whites were counted – there were 2.5 million then – cows were counted, but black people were not, even though they numbered something like 30 to 35 million. They were hardly considered human by most whites. And the official national languages were English and Afrikaans, even though the majority spoke other languages.

Everyone was affected, and infected, by this situation. I remember looking at a newspaper when I was small and reading about an accident. First thought – was the victim white or black? If white, then it was a tragedy. Black – much as if an animal rather than a human being had lost its life. And I was the daughter of rather liberal parents!

From my memories of those early years it is clear I was conditioned to think that blacks were there specifically to serve the whites, in their homes (we had one 'coloured' – mixed race – servant when poor, two when better off) and in the economy. And so it was in practice. In my father's small clothing factory colour differentiation was very precise: the handful of whites, my father and brothers, attracted the profits; the skilled workers, engineers, cutters, were 'coloured' – descendants of long-ago colonial and native liaisons – or Malay; and the unskilled labourers were native blacks, looked down upon by all their 'superiors'. All this seemed so natural to whites.

Then, in the white community itself there was strong prevalent racism, not only between the two main groups, 'English' people and 'Afrikaners', but against the Jews, of whom there were a few hundred thousand. They were mostly immigrants from the pogroms (anti-Semitic riots) of Russia, its territories, and other East European countries. There were 100,000 Lithuanian Jews in the country and this included my parents. Although Jews considered themselves 'English' South Africans, not 'Afrikaners', this was no protection from the anti-Semitism against them in the English and Afrikaner population.

In 1939, for example, with news emanating from Germany of the Nazi oppression of the Jews, which a large number of Afrikaners endorsed, Cape Town docks had a revealing incident. One of the last boats to save refugee Jews from Germany wished to dock in the port to replenish its supplies of food and other requirements. The 100 percent white South African government refused to allow this and Afrikaner street demonstrations endorsed this decision. Jews cowered in their houses while the boat, unreplenished, had to sail elsewhere. I never discovered where. Perhaps the new Jewish congregation founded in North China consisted of these refugees.

South Africa

To counter such attitudes Jews tried to avoid being the object of animosity. They couldn't do much if they had a long nose (except that a few did have an operation to shorten their noses), but they could reduce the volume of their speaking voices and conceal other aspects of their Jewishness. In retrospect to deny one's own identity was quite ridiculous, and so in the other direction Jews cohered as a national body and conducted their lives separately from the other nationalities, with their own Jewish groceries, butchers, dairies and other consumer outlets, their denunciation of 'Christian' holidays like Christmas, and excessive celebration of 'Jewish' holidays. I remember being convinced of the awfulness of Christmas and the joys of Hanukah, which took place at the same time.

Being myself white and Jewish, I was simultaneously a beneficiary and victim of racism, and hence very aware of what nonsensical behavioural impact it could have: talking with a non-Oxford English accent put you at the bottom of the ladder of shame; talking with the hands or walking with the feet pointing outwards were to be avoided. These are the ones I remember most clearly. I was particularly lucky my mother spoke good English without a foreign accent (not so my father, who ate his food out of a 'boil' rather than a bowl). My parents' other 'Jewish' characteristics were not very pronounced. In later years this sensitivity to anti-Jewish racism helped me to understand black people's feelings and their consequent efforts at Europeanising their characteristics: straightening their hair, lightening their skin, and so on.

Life was full of prejudices, prohibitions and taboos. I

went to school when six years old – a whites only, girls only, school. My mother took me there to register, and when asked what my name was, invented one on the spot. I had been called after my grandmother, whose name was the Biblical Hannah, which in Hebrew was Chanah. As most names in South Africa ended in an 'ie' sound it had become Chanie. My mother must have thought this too 'foreign' for an English school, and on the spot anglicised my name to Anetta. That was what I was called throughout my school days, and is now on my birth certificate, although Chanie is what I am called by those who know me.

I remember doing arithmetic one day, pencil in right hand, left hand between my thighs – what many kids do when stressed or embarrassed, as we all were, having just begun school. The teacher, a spinster (married women were not allowed to teach at the time), walked round the class, not marking the work, hardly looking at it in fact, but sedulously removing each child's left hand from her genitals, telling her not to put it there. This was more important than arithmetic.

From the beginning we had tests and class places. I was deemed 'clever', and was consistently top of the class, and therefore seated somewhere at the back, with the other 'clever' children. However, I fell one day, hurt my head and have to have six stitches. This was just before the exams, and I got a very poor mark, near the bottom of the class, and had to sit in the front near the teacher (who did say it must have been because of the accident). I shall never forget how humiliated I felt, and much later realised how those accustomed to be in that lowly position must always have felt. My reaction

South Africa

was to rebel, a reaction I seemed to develop against all insults and humiliations. I became 'naughty' and the teacher threatened to hit me with a ruler. This incensed me even more and I refused to talk to the teacher. However, punishment only lasted for one term as my grades improved and I returned to sitting at the back.

In the secondary school, called The Good Hope Seminary, the 'clever' pupils were taught Latin as a foreign language, the 'not clever' ones French. I therefore came out of school knowing English, Afrikaans (both compulsory), Hebrew and Latin – which left me without any modern continental European language, a big problem when travelling later in Europe. I also learned elocution and starred in public school plays, much to the delight of my family. I was very remiss in not having any close friends in my early school years. I went around with my elder sister Ruth (nicknamed Rochie) who had many close friends. At the age of 11 I realised my friendlessness and decided to look for a mate or special friend. I found another friendless girl called Jean Lemonsky, and although not enraptured by her personality, became her friend. She played the piano, but not half as well as my sister Rochie.

The clear picture of my world as a child was that we Jews were an inferior breed of human beings, and blacks were not human at all. With hindsight it is clear that the resultant confusion of emotions created by these national and racial stereotypes moulded my future attitudes. Teachers told me (subtly, unintentionally but unquestionably) that we were inferior. My mother told me we were the Chosen

People. Being only a kid I believed them both. So to preserve self-respect I had to balance national inferiority with proof of national superiority – bending the stick right over. Great rebelliousness at school was motivated by one thought: 'I'll show 'em who's better!' Whatever I could do to get Jews chosen for school honours I did. Arguing the merits of great Jews of the past with a teacher led to my being put in the corner with my feet in the waste paper basket – which simply egged me on to greater cussedness.

The advent of a Jewish teacher was a huge emotional event. On the one hand, of course, she was inferior – all Jews were – on the other our great love and efforts on her behalf would make her superior. I worked for her as for no one else; all my best creative work at school was done for her in the brief period she taught us.

What propped up my childish pride was the tight-knit, defensive Jewish community, the only place a Jewish child felt wanted, was important and got the emotional nourishment to stand up at school and fight.

In due course I became an extreme and militant Jewish nationalist. The prevailing nationalism was Zionism, which my mother was quite fanatical about. I went to my first Zionist meeting at the age of nine. Committed to fighting tooth and nail against anti-Semitic indignities and to criticising those who failed to do so (usually for financial gain), I was very religious too. That was part of the prop to human dignity.

This childish rebellion against racist injustice was a major influence in my development, and indeed that of nearly all the small band of my compatriots who later became revolutionary socialists. A significant proportion of the whites in left wing organisations

South Africa

were Jewish, and the earliest rebellion of many of these against racist prejudice was extreme Jewish nationalism and religious fervour, expressed as Zionism. But that was not the end of the story. It was a short and logical step, mostly taken between the ages of 13 and 18, for the victims of one national oppression to feel for the victims of another – the blacks. This in turn led us to try and understand the causes of national and racial oppression, and hence later to break the ties with Zionism which was, as we later saw, an oppressive nationalism of its own.

There is a line of argument in the feminist movement that 'the personal is political'. This has often ended up as a way of dividing working class women and men, a grave mistake when liberation depends on a united struggle. So although I do not subscribe to that approach, there are political dynamics at play in families which often take shape around issues such as cooperation or competition, authoritarianism or freedom. As far as my siblings were concerned, we all very much respected Reggie, the eldest, and adored Mikey, the baby, and Mickey above him, who was an exceptionally sweet-tempered child and my father's favourite, insofar as he could show this, by having her on his lap and spending time with her.

The family bully was Alec, the second child. He would throw books at us if he got in a temper, but his worst crime in my eyes was his 'stealing' of my bath. To have a hot bath in those days one had to find pieces of wood, put them into the geyser with paper, light it, and replenish it periodically. This took nearly an hour, and only then could one have a hot bath. Alec, on one occasion, crept into the bathroom when my bath water was already hot, and locked the door. He stole my bath and I, of course, was furious, but to no avail. I had to wait another week before I could have my next bath. The bath stealer went on to affect others outside the family.

When I left school I worked for a time in my father's factory, as a wages clerk. Here, as in all other factories, wages were paid to the nearest 'tickey' (3p). I always put them up to the higher tickey. Alec, who with Reggie helped manage the factory, learnt about this and went and told my father, expecting him to discipline me into taking the wage to the *nearest* tickey, downwards if necessary. My father, thankfully, ignored him and I carried on as before, to Alec's chagrin. In other ways too he sought to prevent the workers' conditions improving. Reggie decided to introduce 'music while you work'. Alec disapproved. There were many other differences between them, with Reggie always liberal and Alec always nasty.

My reaction was not to speak to Alec, and I persevered with this for 30 years till, much older, retired and ill, he came for a visit to England. I then ventured to speak to him, particularly as he had forgotten we were on bad terms and why,

On coming to England, where the majority do not live in tight national communities, I found that many people do not understand that one nationalism is not the same as another. One expresses oppression by the dog, the other the rebellion of the underdog. One fights to preserve inequality, the other to achieve equality. They are opposites. One can lead on to fascist thinking, the other to revolutionary socialism, which destroys national inequality and racism altogether.

South Africa

It was after such early experiences, and because of them, that books entered our lives, to confirm our awakening horror at the human relations about us, to explain the reasons why, to give hope and dream of the brotherhood of and equality of people, and to stimulate us to action to achieve it. We gobbled up all political books and socialist novels available, early becoming Marxists and turning against religion and bourgeois Zionism. There is no one book I would pick out of the welter of them. They collectively consolidated what our circumstances had shaped us into. But it was the circumstances, first and foremost, which shaped us.

The road to revolutionary socialism for us youthful rebels took us through many strange events. For example, I chose to travel third class on the train (for blacks), instead of first class (for whites), or second (for coloureds). The white guard, shocked, pushed me out to the first class compartment in spite of my protests. He did not demand the difference in the price of the ticket, but he did insist on the colour bar being kept. The blacks were incredulous.

But it was hard to be immune to the racist environment. My mother had drilled her children in the religion of sanitary precautions. In every crack of every cup used by blacks lurked syphilis, tuberculosis and other dread scourges. (My mother didn't consider herself a racist – she was hygienic!) I got to know a young Indian man (Indians were considered black), who invited me to a black cafe. I was served tea in a cracked cup and was nearly sick. I finished it as I did not want to upset my host. A second cup was better and no horrible disease ensued.

On one occasion I met a number of acquaintances in Johannesburg, some of whom were black. Five of us walked together down a main street in the centre of town, four black men and me. The white pedestrians were absolutely amazed and stopped dead in their tracks to stare.

Active anti-racism meant the police eventually got on my track and I subsequently left the country. My best friend, who stayed on, spent nine years in prison. It was only years later in England that for the first time I could talk to black and coloured South Africans frankly. Those who had managed to get out were the favoured few. Yet one told me that as a girl in a family with seven children she spoke to only four of her brothers and sisters – the dark four – because the lighter ones were 'playwhites', that is, they mixed with white people in white places and would not greet their darker brothers and sisters, or parents, in the street for fear of discovery of their origins. Another, a bright boy who managed to be one of the 20 blacks to get to university, tried to learn mathematics, physics and chemistry. The latter two being practical subjects, he needed a partner to work with. A white student was found willing to partner him in physics, so he was able to study that subject. A chemistry partner could not be found – so no chemistry. In the maths engineering class (for intending gold mine managers) any row of seats the black student sat in immediately emptied.

White co-workers would talk to a black laboratory assistant in the laboratory, but not even greet her outside in public. Waiting for a boat to come to England, months passed before whites could be found who would share a cabin with a black student. A black worker on a train was arrested by the white steward when he opened a book in a spare moment – how dare the upstart presume to be educated? Black or coloured people could not go into a library to get a book, had to sit on a separate bench to whites in train stations, could not go into public swimming pools, 'white' hotels, and so on and so on. If the ban was not official, as many were, it was thoroughly enacted unofficially.

Rebellion also included the emotional world. Although my mother warned me to be careful around boys and I was, it was not nearly as strictly as she hoped for. I started indulging in sexual experience. My first 'love' was called Paul. From Rhodesia, he was holidaying in Muizenberg, a beach suburb of Cape Town. We mostly held hands and went sightseeing. I missed him terribly when he went home, and didn't eat for three days. I had two other contemporaneous 'loves' in Hashomer Hatzair, the militant Zionist youth movement, before leaving for Palestine – Baruch Hirson and Chaim Goldsmith, who were very jealous of each other. They were both very different, and I liked them for their different characteristics. In later life Baruch became an academic and wrote books on South African history. Chaim went into his family's business and social life. But I cannot say I really 'loved' either of them and when I later left for Palestine in 1944 at the age of 22 I felt emotionally free.

My parents, like all parents, wanted me to find a job that earned good money, so they apprenticed me to my uncle who was an accountant, and entered me at Cape Town University to study accountancy and other business studies. I detested this proposed career and wrote essays for the economics course as a Marxist socialist. Our lecturer duly strongly discredited my views and awarded bad marks. I gradually ceased going to the classes, and instead spent time in the arts department of the university which had a very good general and also arts library. I became very interested in art, which had been a hobby since the age of about 11. My father smoked, and in each box of cigarettes he bought was a copy of a famous painting which was to go into a book about art and artists. There were a hundred spaces, and I eventually filled them all, in the process learning a lot about painting. I investigated Renaissance art and artists, moved on to the Impressionists and modern movements, and was fascinated by Soviet revolutionary art. (At that time we still thought Soviet Russia was a socialist – or communist – country.) I also fell in love with Diego Rivera, the great Mexican artist, kept copies of his paintings and even tried to copy his style myself when painting the walls of the room in Cape Town in which we had held our Hashomer Hatzair meetings.

My attitude to art changed and developed with time. I felt that the magnificent Renaissance artistic revolution, where painting was realistic, ended with the arrival of the camera, abstract art starting to take its place. I had tried throughout my life to find out why I appreciated or liked a picture. What particular characteristic caused this to be the case? I became interested in abstract art and sought, by going to exhibitions and examining work in art books, to learn to understand and appreciate it. This took a long time, many years in fact. If I become acquainted with a picture over a long period of time it begins to 'speak' to me, not in words, but in thoughts and feelings. I can then relate to it in detail and discover, for the

South Africa

particular picture, why I like or dislike it. Personally I find definite shapes in a picture make more sense to me than a wishy washy slithering of the paintbrush. Definiteness seems to 'speak' more to me, which is perhaps why I began sculpting in hard materials during retirement.

Driving – in South Africa and beyond

Driving would be important in my later political life. Cliff never learned to do that and so I had to become a chauffeur for him, and for myself, in my role as an activist and family builder. I learned to drive in South Africa where racism influenced everything. In my case it produced an unexpected turn of events – literally.

I am not a natural when it comes to driving and had to try three times before getting a license. I was asked one day to get a car to a certain place. As it had no engine it could not, however, be driven. Foolishly I agreed to do this, with a friend driving a car behind, shunting. We managed alright till I had to turn right. When I was in the middle of the turn I saw a car coming full speed at me, and I could do nothing to move out of the way. The other car drove straight into mine. I was not hurt, nor was anyone in the other car, but my car had to be moved to the side of the road.

The accident led to a court case which testified to racist (and sexist) justice in South Africa. The magistrate was a South African Englishman, the other car's driver an Afrikaner. This would be significant in court because the English were pre-eminent in South African business, while the Afrikaners dominated agriculture, but wanted to gain control in business also. This caused dissension. The case was heard in English except for the Afrikaner who refused an English translator. The magistrate decided to look at the site of the accident, which meant his sitting beside me, young and 'beautiful' as I was then, in the back of an official car. I did my utmost to win the magistrate over to my side in the case, and of course did not divulge that the vehicle I had driven had no engine. The magistrate did not discover this fact as he did not bother to open up the engine. When we got back to court there was no question that the Afrikaner would lose the case, whose outcome was entirely due to national antagonism between the English and Afrikaners, and my youth and spoken language.

There is one driving experience I am famous – or infamous – for. Decades later I was driving slowly along a London side street not far from home when a council bin worker, his view obscured by a bin on his shoulder, walked between two parked cars into my path. I could not stop in time and knocked him over, his full bin spilling all over the street. His arm was injured and he was taken to hospital where I went to visit him. While there I recruited him to the Socialist Workers Party.

As a friend said, this was not a lesson in driving ability, but in recruitment possibilities. My family have always considered me an unsafe driver and tried to get me to stop driving. I have at last given in, and now drive only a mobility scooter, which I find very handy.

Part 2
Palestine

With my parents being adamant Zionists and having all their seven children learn Hebrew from the age of five, I early adopted Zionism as my politics. At 15 I met a woman who came to South Africa from a kibbutz in Palestine. There were a larger number of kibbutzim in Palestine in different groups, accommodating different left wing political organisations. This woman was from a Hashomer Hatzair (Young Guard) kibbutz. Hashomer Hatzair was on the extreme left wing of Zionism. She described the kibbutz to me thus:

First of all, and crucially, there was no money in the kibbutz. Its members, anything from about 300 to 1,000 or more, simply received all their requirements – living quarters, food, health requirements, cultural events, etc – from the kibbutz, and these conditions they voted on themselves. Every decision was arrived at in a kibbutz meeting of all its members. I remember a decision being taken about the daily number of hours members should work. I moved eight hours; someone else moved nine. Nine won, and that is what we worked.

Work was rotated wherever possible, so that everyone did the good jobs and the rotten jobs. We all had two sets of clothes, one for work and one for leisure, which we chose from the laundered washing. So we could, if we wished, have different clothes every week. That was how life was in the Hashomer Hatzair kibbutz at the time. Things are very different in the kibbutzim as a whole today, as, inevitably, the outside capitalist market world has influenced the kibbutz economy. The new generation largely works outside the kibbutz, receiving different individual wages, hence contributing different amounts and receiving different amounts from the kibbutz. This has played a part in money being used by members in many kibbutzim, and jobs not being rotated. Kibbutz habits of living have therefore largely changed, more nearly approaching the habits of the outside world, such as paying for meals and services. The politics of Zionist occupation has also had a corroding effect, but more of that later.

I was thrilled by the account of life in Hashomer Hatzair kibbutzim, immediately became a Zionist socialist, and not long after joined Hashomer Hatzair in Cape Town and later Johannesburg. In preparation for going to a kibbutz in Palestine, I worked with my other comrades on a farm near Johannesburg, taught by a farmer.

The journey to Palestine by boat along the East African coast was hellishly hot and threatened with Japanese bombs as the war was on. When we got to Egypt I was amazed at the customs officer who investigated our luggage. He looked at my large box of books – all basic Marxist texts – and spent the whole day reading them.

In Palestine I joined a preparatory Hashomer Hatzair kibbutz in the north of the country, which was one of four kibbutzim at the base of a hill, on the other side of which were four Palestinian Arab villages, each with its own head man. In those days, before the state of Israel was formed, the Zionists paid for land bought from the Palestinians, and the four Palestinian villages were thus duly sold to the kibbutzim. However, when the day came to receive the land, which was a few weeks before I arrived, the Palestinian farmers refused to leave – naturally, as the payment had been pocketed by the head men and the farmers received nothing. The kibbutz members thereupon decided to climb the hill, picking up stones as they went, and threw them at the Palestinians, who fled. I was told about this event long after my arrival. I realised that it was not only the Jewish National Fund, government, and businessmen who stole the Palestinian lands and evicted their inhabitants, but also the 'socialist' kibbutzim. The internal collaborative and progressive nature of such kibbutzim was a means of uniting people to act externally to occupy and expropriate the lands of others. It was a cruel fraud.

About a dozen of us Hashomer Hatzair comrades had travelled to Palestine together. On arrival we wanted a local Zionist socialist to come and speak to us and introduce us to the left wing politics of the community. We were offered this young man whose main characteristic was a huge shock of black hair. He duly came, as we finished work at 2pm on a Friday afternoon, and started speaking, and went on and on without stopping in a Hebrew no one understood. I knew more Hebrew than the others, and I was at a complete loss. At midnight he stopped and asked, 'Does anyone want to ask any questions, or say anything?' After waiting a few moments he declared, 'Hurry up, you're wasting time,' and went on speaking till 4am, at which point, exhausted, we all went to bed. This was Ygael Gluckstein. Later on, in England, we would not be called by his family name, but took the name Tony Cliff. For simplicity the name Cliff is used throughout.

Shortly after this I received a request to help translate a leaflet into English for the British troops in Palestine. It meant going to Tel Aviv and working with Cliff who wrote the leaflet. We worked solidly for three days, after which I said, 'Can't we go for a walk or something?' to which he replied, 'What? Waste time?' But we did, in fact, go for a walk and got to know each other. Cliff was attracted by my South African passport. Bolstered by this and possibly some other useful characteristics, we starting living together.

Wedding

Eventually we had to get married. We could not have travelled together if we were not married, as Cliff had a rotten British Mandate passport, and I had a good South African one. So we made preparations for the marriage, which perforce had to be numerous, for a number of reasons.

In the first place Cliff was married, in the same way as a very large number of other young Jewish men were, as a means of saving the lives of young Jewish women from Nazi Germany. Before the Second World War ships managed to fill with Jewish women oppressed by the Nazis and some made their way to Palestine. There the Jewish men stood on the pier, each took a woman and they were married by a rabbi who was party to the action. The couple then shook hands and went their separate ways. But to get married again they had to divorce, and this the rabbis were not party to as they had been with marriages. So Cliff had to find his 'wife' to divorce her. He had no idea where to look. His father, however, continued the search and eventually did manage to find her. Cliff duly got divorced.

Now arose the question of the wedding ceremony. We had no money to speak of, hence could not hire an indoor venue for the occasion. So we adopted the behaviour of the poor and had the 'chupah' (canopy) on the pavement surrounded by expectant beggars.

The next problem was Cliff's clothes. His entire possessions, besides his books, were a pair of short trousers, a pair of sandals and a shift. For a wedding you at least need long trousers, and for a Jewish ceremony something to cover the crown of the head. By good luck we had a South African friend who had long trousers. The only problem was that he was half Cliff's size, so that Cliff could not close his trousers at the waist. A 'hat' he borrowed from a building worker relative – in other words, a slouch cap, defaced by cement. This was how he was dressed for his wedding. I wore my work clothes, consisting of a navy blue shirt and skirt.

According to ancient custom the wedding is the first time the groom sees the face of the bride, who therefore has to wear a veil to cover her face. My sister-in-law gave me a pretty net. 'No,' said the rabbi, 'her face can be seen.' So my sister-in-law gave me the only other thing she had – a handkerchief – and with this I walked several times round Cliff, as prescribed by the marriage law. The ring was also borrowed from my sister-in-law. Needing to be of value, most wedding rings are made of gold. But not this one. 'What's this?' asked the rabbi. Cliff had previously asked the same question, so he knew the answer. 'Platinum,' he said. The rabbi had not heard of platinum, so in the middle of the marriage ceremony he asked, 'How much did it cost?' Cliff gave a suitably high figure.

With our last coins we had bought a bottle of wine, hoping later to offer it to my brother and his wife who attended, really to help with our requirements. The wine, at least, was ours. What did the rabbi do about this? He put a glass to our lips and then kept the rest of the bottle – stole it in fact. As soon as the ceremony was over, all the beggars put their hands out, pleading for 'backsheesh', which my brother provided with all the money he had in his pocket. But we couldn't offer my brother a glass of wine!

Our wedding 'feast' was provided by a friend who worked in a restaurant and was allowed to take home the food that was starting to go off. We loved it, having nothing better! I then went off to work, in a canning factory, and Cliff to change into his more comfortable short trousers. Fortunately I had told all my relatives, besides my brother, not to attend our wedding as they would have been shocked by our poverty. My brother and his wife were well mannered enough not to show what they thought!

Palestine

Cliff had organised a group of 20 to 30 anti-Zionist revolutionary socialists, both Arab and Jewish. Its main Palestinian member was Jabra Nicola, who was the vice-editor of a daily Arabic paper. This job did not deliver him much of a living, as I found out when I had to go to his abode in Jaffa to pick up an article for our paper. He lived in one room, with his wife and baby and four other adult relatives who were sleeping in available beds on the floor. We all shared poverty, though we did manage to collect money for Fourth International candidates in different national elections. This meant going without a meal or two for our poverty-stricken comrades. Cliff and Jabra spent hours together, often wandering along the beach the whole night, evaluating and promoting the politics of our small organisation.

Our politics had to start from scratch in the early 1940s. Stalinism was showing its anti-revolutionary nature, endorsing what it called socialism in one country (Russia alone), through its labour camps, its opposition to and murder of all the 1917 revolutionary leaders, and its restrictions and persecution of the workers and smaller nationalities. Trotsky kept alive the ambitions of the 1917 Russian Socialist Revolution, in particular the impossibility of socialism in one country, averring that it could only exist internationally and had to be fought for thus.

It was therefore natural that our group became Trotskyist and that Cliff and Jabra developed Trotskyist politics. The organisation they built affiliated to the Fourth International, a Trotskyist current opposed to Stalinism in Russia. Eventually Cliff went further than Trotskyist orthodoxy, proclaiming Russia to be state capitalist – not Communist or a degenerated workers' state.

Leaving the kibbutz after six months and living with Cliff in Tel Aviv, I got a job as a governess to a very rich South African businessman's granddaughter. This confirmed my beliefs. She expressed a liking for rich children as opposed to the poor on the grounds that they could have what they wanted. I breakfasted with the grandfather. On his side of the breakfast table were quality white bread, butter, coffee, fish, etc; on my side inferior brown bread, margarine, tea and nothing else. He would pass me in a car going into town while I walked, and not offer me a lift.

There was a cellar in the house which the grandfather never entered. There I hid our leaflets, one of which was supporting a combined Jewish-Arab strike in a British refinery. The leaflet was written in Hebrew on one side and Arabic on the other. For some unknown reason the grandfather came into the cellar, saw the leaflets, and I immediately got the sack.

I then went into teaching English in adult and children's classes, though was always horrified to hear my strong South African English accent coming out of the pupils' mouths. My earnings enabled us to live, if poorly.

The highlight of our time was a meal of camel meat (the cheapest meat available) once a month in a restaurant. Largely we lived off fruit, mainly oranges, which we picked off trees for free in the nearby orchards. Our accommodation was half a basement room in a very large building, the other half consisting of the electrical and other machinery for the building. The bed and wardrobe we acquired took up all the width of the room, and the bed had to be sat upon for the wardrobe to open. We did actually have our own toilet which proved very useful whenever the British troops or police came searching, which was not infrequently, as we could flush away our illegal literature.

Before I came to the country Cliff had been in prison for a year for having written an illegal revolutionary socialist leaflet. We didn't want a repeat of that. And in fact when we did get arrested and dumped in a tennis court under a blazing sun (together with hundreds of other 'criminals', most of whom were fighting for the creation of the Jewish state), my ability to speak the English language to the English police and my good South African passport got both of us liberated.

Our group produced a newspaper which had a different name with each issue, as each one was banned. It was *Workers' Voice* or *Workers' Life* or *Workers' Concerns* or whatever. Being illegal, its printing and distribution were difficult. Danny Tait was the brave comrade who took the written sheets to the printers, from Tel Aviv to Haifa. The coach he travelled on was usually stopped and searched by the police. Danny worked out a method of hiding his written sheets so that they were not revealed, and with luck aiding his good sense he was never caught. Distribution of the paper was a problem. One way we did this was to climb to the top of a building in a busy street and throw the leaflets down to the pavement below. People picked them up and read them. I had a particular distribution job – to get the paper to the students at the Hebrew University. I waited for the common room to be empty, dumped the papers and ran. I was never caught.

Chanie and Cliff outside Buckingham Palace after their arrival in London, 1946

Fighting fit: A memoir

Cliff,
Chanie
d Elana
njoy the
garden

Part 3
Britain & Europe

My mother and father, younger sister and brother (Miriam, known as Mickey, and Michael, known as Mikey) came to Palestine about now. In 1946 Cliff and I were married and decided to leave Palestine to travel to Europe, mainly because he felt the need to live in a country which had world-class libraries like the British Museum in London. But this was not at all straightforward. Foreign travel in the British Mandate was under the control of a British commissioner, who was the only one who could give permission to travel abroad at the time. My father, who owned a small clothing factory in Cape Town, thought he needed a visa to go to England, which he intended to visit via Palestine, in order to buy material for his factory. He gave his visa to Cliff when he found out he, as a South African, did not need one. So the commissioner was the person I had to intercede with on Cliff's behalf. I dressed in my finest clothes, complete with hat, gloves, etc, all in one colour, green, as I remember.

As usual, the commissioner, like the other British officials, was happy to have a conversation in properly spoken English, and I obtained permission for Cliff to travel. In 1946 we took a boat from Haifa to Marseilles in France. Other than Cliff losing his glasses overboard on our journey and his consequent despair at his potential inability to visit the Moulin Rouge we had heard so much about, all went well till we got to Marseilles. We had been told that France, owing to the war, had no blades for men to shave with, and that we could manage well financially if we took plenty of blades with us to sell. We spent a lot of our small finances on blades, but when we got to France discovered that French men had as many blades as they needed. As usual we lost out money-wise.

But we became very busy politically, as the Trotskyist International Secretariat met in Paris. The Trotskyist movement was small and there was no country in which it could organise large-scale working class activities. At the same time the Communist parties were surging ahead, aligning the economic and political systems of Eastern Germany and other East European countries with Soviet Russia's so-called Communist regime. This was the headline news, and the Trotskyist Fourth International was reduced to small, ineffective national groups.

Unfortunately the members of the International Secretariat were hardly mature enough to appreciate their political ineffectiveness, and behaved in a make-believe fashion which very much put us off, we who had come from one of the world's most politically difficult countries. We were in Paris for only a few days, but they kept us waiting for hours while they typed away on their typewriters, in an attempt to impress us about how busy they were. And what got us even more upset was that they somehow managed to get food and drink unobtainable to ordinary French workers at the time at the end of the war – milk, coffee, etc. Cliff had a relative in Paris with a young child, so we knew the difficulty in getting healthy food.

A proposal made to Cliff was that, as he knew a few languages, he should stay for the Fourth International conferences to translate for the different nationalities. Cliff was totally averse to this proposal so we moved on to London.

When we arrived we were nearly refused entry by the British. As noted, Cliff was travelling on my dad's visa to buy material in Britain for his factory. The immigration official asked Cliff what was the name of the factory he represented to buy the material in Britain, and he did not know it! I was aghast, but quickly managed to unearth a letter with the required heading – Montrose – and the official accepted this. The immigration officials gave Cliff only three months permission to stay in Britain and ordered him to report to the police every week.

Cliff had met a British MP, Campbell Stephen, who had visited Palestine, and he spoke up for him and enabled him to prolong his stay beyond the three months. He eventually needed another letter from the MP in order not to be deported. We then heard that Campbell Stephen was very ill, in fact dying. We found out the address at which he was staying – a village in the country – and rushed there. We knocked on the door and a nurse opened it. We asked her to get the MP to sign the letter we had written on his behalf. She confirmed that he was on his deathbed and could not do it. But we were desperate, and eventually she was persuaded to try and get the signature. We did get it, and Cliff was able to stay longer in England, until the time the authorities decided to deport him. Cliff had been notified by every country to which he had applied to go that he was not welcome, they no doubt having been informed of his previous imprisonment. I even went to France to contact its foreign office to try and get him accepted. This was 1946, and the clerk I spoke to (in English, as my French is useless) had clearly learnt English during the Second World War and wanted to go on practising it. He spoke to me for a solid hour in English, ending with the words, 'Phone me again in an hour.' I duly did so. This time the conversation lasted ten seconds: 'Your husband will NEVER come to France.'

Every other country except Ireland gave the same answer. The Irish hated the British government, which had acted for centuries as their imperialist occupier. They were consequently prepared to accept Cliff. More than that, when he arrived, the immigration official he dealt with smacked him on his shoulder and said, 'Congratulations, old man,' meaning 'Good that you Palestinians are fighting the British.'

We found the Trotskyists in Britain much better than the International Secretariat in France. They did not try to make believe about the class struggle. For example, they were connected with apprentices in Scotland who came out on an important strike, and this energised them enormously.

London introduced me to something I had never seen in South Africa – snowfall. On Christmas Day in my first year in London I went outside to see the children playing with their new scooters and toys. While there it started snowing. I could hardly believe how beautiful it was to see the flakes drifting down. I was completely transfixed by this heavenly artistry and stood there throughout the snowstorm with the flakes falling all over me. To this day I still think it the most glorious of sights and will stare wonderingly at a snowstorm from its beginning to its end without moving.

At the chalk face

I decided to take up teaching. I had a BA degree in Hebrew from Cape Town University. Even though this had absolutely nothing to do with school teaching, the degree enabled me to apply to be a teacher in Islington. I expected to be sent on a course, but no, I was told to teach infants there and then. I knew nothing about schools in England and said I couldn't do it. 'Have you got two legs to stand on?' asked the official. On my positive reply he said, 'Then you teach infants', and I was appointed to a school. The education authorities were so desperate over the shortage of teachers after the war that a degree in Hebrew and two legs to stand on were sufficient to make a teacher out of an educational ignoramus. I was quite distraught and decided to join courses for every aspect of infant teaching, covering the whole syllabus over two years. Only then did I feel I was a proper teacher.

It was a rewarding job. My headmistress introduced me to a non-phonetic reading scheme called 'Look and Say', which I found very rewarding. This method meant learning seven short sentences (attached to pictures) by heart, then matching the seven up with strips, repeating them, then cutting the sentences up into words and matching each word on the original sentences. So the children learnt to recognise the 27 words which were all that were used in the first reading book of the series. The child was then given this first book, and read right through it, to his or her extreme delight, and subsequently the child's parents. I too was delighted to hear the child read right through the book unaided, as I had previously tried to teach reading by the phonic method, and found it extremely difficult, almost impossible with some children. The government today is seeking to impose a single rigid method on teachers for reading. I really enjoyed teaching reading to infants, but doubt if that would be the case today.

Another area of my work was painting. As a class we would discuss what we intended to paint, for example a windy day, and after all the children's ideas had been put forward, we would settle down to do the painting. I find children's paintings fascinating, and I sent some of my class's paintings to various children's exhibitions, where a few were accepted, to our great delight. I taught infants for many years. In so doing I became interested in education – the way children, and people in general, learn, relations between teachers and pupils, including the physical layout of a classroom, the effects of different class sizes, and so on.

The advantage of teaching infants things like reading

and painting is that they have not yet had the spontaneity or creativity crushed out of them. But, unfortunately, that is the purpose of education under capitalism (at least for the working class kids). For that reason I never learnt to love teaching. In the present circumstances of bourgeois society there is a requirement (and a survival need given class numbers) to maintain a permanently quiet class, that is to 'keep order', where the adults were the only ones with the prerogative to decide on this 'order'. 'Order' is something kept by a so-called superior over inferiors. I never felt superior as a person to anyone, old or young. I therefore could not wholeheartedly desire to subdue the class permanently while I taught them. Children like to learn and I thought that without speaking they would not learn as well as they would if they could discuss the subject being taught while it was being taught. But as my infant classes usually numbered as many as 42, the question of keeping order while teaching played a large part in shaping my evolving attitude to the job.

So after teaching infants for 15 years I decided I might be happier teaching secondary pupils, where perhaps 'order' could be less onerous. I therefore joined a teachers' mathematics teaching class. I had been good at mathematics while at school, and there was a desperate shortage of maths teachers. After passing my exam I got a maths teaching job in Hackney. The question of 'order' did not change much from infant teaching, and my headmistress presumed I would not be able to teach maths satisfactorily. However, in my first year at the school the whole class passed the GCSE, getting mostly As and Bs, a few Cs and one D. The headmistress was surprised and very commendatory, and it did in fact enable me to talk more amicably with the children, so that 'order' was not so strict. In fact, when we went out on strike, beginning in 1969, we spent a whole lesson discussing the issue. The children supported the teachers' demand for a good London allowance wholeheartedly and some came with us when we marched during the strike. I spent 12 years teaching maths at the one school, John Howard, in Laura Place in Hackney.

I continued my interest in educational theory and practice and helped build a Rank and File teachers' group, which supported left wing union action and also educational theory. We held an education conference for which I wrote the introductory paper, and this was subsequently printed as a pamphlet called *Education and Society*. It covered the aims of education, the physical framework for these aims, ideas for change, forces for change and lastly socialist education. At a later conference I wrote the blurb again and called it *Education and Revolution*. This too became a pamphlet. I also helped to write a pamphlet on salaries, another on classrooms and teaching areas, all of which was much later incorporated into a booklet written by me and Kevin Ovenden, who at the time wrote the articles on education in *Socialist Worker*. Such activities did not only meet opposition from school managements. At an NUT conference in the early 1970s held after I had written the pamphlets, Max Morris, a Communist Party member and one of the best known members of the NUT National Executive, got up after I had put up my hand to ask a question of the chair and denounced me roundly. The conference was aghast, as such an aggressive tone had not been used before, and announced that Max Morris was to apologise or not return to conference after lunch. He was not there after lunch; apologise he certainly would not. I became secretary of the 12,000 strong Hackney branch of the National Union of Teachers in 1969. Teachers at that time were very badly paid and large numbers of them took on another job besides teaching, particularly in London, where living cost more than elsewhere. Our Rank and File group decided to push for a London strike to get a London allowance of £300. Teachers had not been involved in any strike for over 40 years – since the General Strike year of 1926.

We had three people, of which I was one, on the Inner London Teachers' Association (ILTA), which met monthly, and in the first month the vote for our strike motion was three. The Communist Party had six members on ILTA, and we decided to try to get them to vote for the strike too. The next month three of the six did, so we got six votes. Meanwhile agitation among the London teachers got a number of the National Executive Committee members also to come over, so that in the third month there was a majority for strike action. This agitation was an education all of its own. We had to organise on a rank and file basis because not only were we up against the educational authorities (with their government backers behind them), but had to overcome the obstacle of the trade union bureaucracy which sits between the working class and the bosses and often tries to dampen down activity and sell out struggles so that it can deliver 'a deal'. Thus, as part of our agitation Rank and File organised an occupation of the main hall at union headquarters by a large number of teachers. The local teachers' associations in London and individual schools were also actively agitating and getting parents and the public to support the teachers.The resultant fortnight's strike was most impressive, with almost all London schools participating, picketing their schools, getting parents and members of the public to sign petitions, and so on. I worked myself to death staying up every night till about 3am writing and printing leaflets, petitions and other material on our union Gestetner printing machine, then rising early in the morning to picket my school and conduct other strike business; so much so that on the thirteenth day I fell ill and had to stay in bed. The next day the strike ended, and we heard that we had won, not £300, but £301 (as the computer machines at the time seemed unable to deal with noughts). After this we were out on strike on and off, nationally, for the next five years, for higher pay. I was teaching at a special school at the time, for special needs children, and our NUT executive had decided that special schools should not participate in the strikes. I could not let this happen, and went and spoke to an executive member, telling him I'd organise to get them out unless the executive withdrew their disclaimer. I won the argument, the executive changed their minds and the special schools came out with the rest. Following this my head came into the staffroom, saying, 'There have been 11 weeks this term, and in every single week there has been a strike or a day, or two or three'. The strikes again were highly successful. The Houghton Award of 1974 introduced a new salary scheme, and everyone's salary increased enormously. The only grouse we had was that head teachers did much better than rank and file teachers. Their salaries went up by many thousands of pounds per annum. The strikes ended in 1974, with all teachers much more aware of working class strike action, pickets, marches – often organised on the spot if there were enough teachers at a particular event. Teachers had become part of the working class, a fighting part when required. This was a dramatic change from earlier times when the profession was regarded as thoroughly 'middle class' and separate from the working class movement. As far as I was concerned, what I learnt in those five years gave me a thorough understating of working class thinking, agitation, push for action for their demands, strikes and negotiations for results. I also learned one useful political lesson: how important an organised political organisation like the SWP is to the struggle. Its members can be relied on when decisions are taken, and can initiate those decisions and fight for them if necessary. The idea for the Rank and File Teacher groups, for example, flowed from our analysis of Russia and state capitalism. Socialism could not be brought from above, but had to come from below, and so the rank and file had to organise itself to bring about change.

This does not mean that all wisdom and leadership are to be found solely within the political organisation. Time and again individuals who had never shown any participation or leadership quality, perhaps never even spoken at meetings, suddenly became strike leaders, unquestioningly taking on all the hard work connected with keeping the strike action alive.Socialists need to be active in their own workplaces and the relevant trade union, but solidarity with others is just as important, because we are not fighting for better pay or conditions, but for a different society, and that requires united action across the working class. That is why there was so much activity during the miners' strike of 1984-85. This including collecting money at school and also in the street with miners who came to the cities precisely for this purpose. We also travelled round the country visiting miners' families while the men were out collecting or propagandising. There were some astonishing contributions full of gifts of food and other resources sent in solidarity by workers in a host of other countries.

Miners stayed with us for weeks at a time. I remember one telling us how he'd eaten at home. His wife brought in a plate of peas for him and their son. When they had finished it he said, 'Thanks. And now the meal?' 'That was the meal,' she said. I learned how much people are ready to suffer for what they believe.

A strike is certainly a most important target that politically shapes the working class and its members. As the well-known saying of a well-known Russian Minister of Internal Affairs goes, 'Every strike discloses the hydra-head of revolution.'

Blacklisting

After the strikes were over I decided to take a sort of holiday and not teach for just one term. I couldn't take more time out as I was the only earner in the family. What I did, in fact the major reason I took the holiday, was to sell a book Cliff wrote, called *The Employers' Offensive*, in the factories in the north-west London Industrial estate which was the largest industrial estate in Europe at the time.

I took the book from factory to factory asking to speak to the union convenor, or if there wasn't one or he was not there, a shop steward. After examining the book, most factories bought half a dozen books, some more, some less. They were all very friendly and I discovered then how well rooted the Communist Party was in the English working class, as practically every shop steward was a Communist Party member, as were the convenors. I came across only one mainly Labour Party factory in the whole area. The book sold thousands of copies and became well known generally in the working class. I heard that at a railway workers' school many of the worker students came to the classes with the book to make sure the tutor imbued them with the ideas they wished to hear. Towards the end of the term I started applying for jobs, and discovered to my horror that I was blacklisted and could get no job in Hackney, where I had been the NUT secretary. My qualifications were excellent. Maths teachers were almost impossible to find in Hackney, and I had spent 12 years successfully teaching maths in the borough's only grammar school. My other long-term experience was teaching infants, also hard to find teachers for at that time. All the head teachers in Hackney knew of me and my doings. I went to my own head and asked her what she had said to the heads, to whose schools I had applied. 'Nothing,' she said, 'only that you were interested in social affairs.' I believed her, but it was enough to get me blacklisted. That result was achieved in many different ways.

In one secondary school, the year six (first year of secondary) teacher had a heart attack and the pupils were left without a class teacher. The school wanted the class taught by primary school methods. My experience was perfect for the job, and the deputy head who was interviewing me actually got down on his knees, put his hands together in prayer fashion and begged me to take it. I asked him not to hassle me, but allow a couple of days to make up my mind. I rang the deputy head two days later to accept the job. All he said was, 'The position is taken,' and put the phone down.

Another school advertised for a maths teacher. I applied, the result: only one applicant, position to be re-advertised. I applied again. The same result: only one application, position to be re-advertised, same result. I subsequently heard that an English teacher at the school was drafted in to teach maths. I, a maths teacher, was blacklisted.

An infant school in Hackney applied for a teacher. I offered my services. The responsible Hackney inspector following the case immediately went to visit the school's new head and told her not to dare to take me on. 'Do you want your school to be run by committee,' she asked, 'or do you want to run it yourself?' Another primary school required four teachers. I decided to apply together with another

51

teacher, a friend, Dorothy McColgan. She also had a history of being upbraided for having fought her school bureaucracy together with a number of other teachers. The reply from this school was that all the positions were taken. By whom – we wondered – the deputy head, the head and two others? There were other laughable – or tragic – blacklisting incidents, all in Hackney, where the inspectors ultimately responsible for filling the teaching position knew me, and didn't like that they knew.

I was becoming a bit desperate, wondering how we and our four children would manage to live. I then applied to a special school – for special needs children – overseen by non-Hackney inspectors who did not know me. There were 13 applicants. I got the job. There could be no better proof of blacklisting than that.

Demonstrations

Alongside trade union activities and strikes, which usually begin over economic issues (though they have the potential to develop in a political direction), demonstrations, which are usually over more general issues, have played an important part in my life. Conventional politics is all about passivity. You are allowed to put a cross on a sheet of paper once every four or five years and then they want you to go back to political sleep. Socialist politics is all about activity, and one manifestation of that is demonstrating.

I went on innumerable demonstrations for a vast variety of causes: against the National Front and subsequent fascist organisations, against the H-bomb, for education causes, over industrial disputes, and so on. In most nothing untoward happened, but not in all.

In one, against the H-bomb, large numbers of the demonstrators sat down in the street. The police, after unsuccessfully exhorting us to get up and go, brought along police vans to throw us into and take us to the police station. Each person was picked up by two policemen. I had very recently had a baby, and was much fatter than my usual self. The policemen looked at me and called up two more so that I had to be carried and thrown into the van by four policemen.

At the police station we were kept for about six hours. At the time I was breastfeeding my baby who was a mere six weeks old. But the police refused to let me go home to feed her. Before letting me go we were told to come to court the next day. This time, to avoid again missing the baby's feed, I decided to take her to court. When I got there I was relieved of the child by a policewoman and was taken into the court, where I was fined £1, if I remember correctly. I then took the baby from the policewoman and fed her in a cell.

The big media workers' (journalists' and printers') strike at Wapping in London in 1986 was another tense time. The support for the strike was huge, as was also the police presence, many of whom were on horseback. Moving among the supporting crowd, I noticed a police horse coming straight at me. I made my way through the crowd as quickly as I could, arriving at the police barriers just as the horse was almost upon me. A couple of strikers on the other side of the barriers grabbed hold of my shoulder and hauled me over the barrier to their side. The policeman went away empty handed. I rapidly recovered from my injuries.

The well known strike of workers at Grunwick's photograph agency in the late 1970s held its picket at 6.30 in the morning, attended by large numbers of supporters. On one occasion Arthur Scargill, the famous general secretary of the miners' union, came to support the picket with hundreds of miners. That was the morning I too went there, intending to go back to work at school later on. It was summer time and I went in a summer dress and sandals. While the strike supporters were crowding the street, an ambulance came along, and the police told the people to move away from the street to let the ambulance through. As previously ambulances had been loaded brimful with policemen come to harass strike supporters, I yelled to the people to stay put. Some did, but many others moved quickly out of the road, and in so doing accidentally knocked me and another girl over. My sandals came off and I fell to the ground in the middle of the road. People were still moving to the pavements, and in doing so many walked over me, bruising me badly. It crossed my mind that I might be going to die or be badly injured, and I felt myself all over to find out if I had any broken bones. However, when I could eventually get up nothing was broken, but I had terrible bruises all over, and a few cuts.

Fighting fit: A memoir

I went to my school, where the first aid was administered by the school secretary who was an extreme right-wing Tory. She was furious with me for supporting the Grunwick's strikers, but she was obliged to see to my cuts and bruises, unwilling as she was. I found myself unable to sit down for almost ten days, but suffered no lasting injuries.

I remember hearing about the Camden (north London) rent strike on the radio, and decided to go there to support the council tenants. There was an astonishing sight when I got there. Women were banging their pots and pans on the balconies, and the police were trying unsuccessfully to get in to arrest one of the leaders. They eventually managed to do this by climbing onto the roof and from there getting into his flat through a window. At night the streets were littered with pots and pans, clothing and other household goods. I picked up a pair of high-heeled shoes, but as I do not wear high heels, I left them where I found them in the street. Another housing demonstration took thousands of us on a march from Hackney to the city hall by the River Thames. There, on the adjacent lawns, we danced and picnicked the whole day. That was a very pleasant demonstration for a good cause.

Over the years I attended many anti-fascist demonstrations. When I came to England in 1946 Oswald Mosley was trying to achieve what Hitler had done in the 1930s and 1940s in Germany. Mosley had been roundly defeated in the East End of London when thousands of Jewish people and Irish workers, the sizeable Communist Party and other left wing organisations came together to prevent his fascists marching down Cable Street, the government of the day having refused to ban his march. Mosley and his fascists were routed then by the large numbers of protesters, who set up barricades throughout the area. He still tried to drum up support later in Ridley Road, where the biggest Hackney market was situated. The market was closed on Sundays, and whoever got to it first on Sunday morning could try to rally the crowds for the rest of the day. Mosley and his fascist sometimes captured the rostrum, other times the left did. When Mosley did, the left met in a nearby street, but their message did not have half the resonance there as in the market place.

On one particular Sunday thousands of protestors came to oppose Mosley's capture of the market rostrum: a very large number of Jews, and all the left wing parties from the Labour Party to the revolutionary groups. Mosley's fascists appeared in an open lorry and tried to enter the market place. They were heavily pelted with rotting fruit and vegetables, so much so that their ducking did not save them from being drenched with the rotting food. The lorry turned round and left. That was the last time the fascists tried to capture the market rostrum.

In 1978 the NF (the nazi National Front) who had just gained over 100,000 votes in London elections, decided to meet in Hyde Park. Our anti-fascists came in large numbers and prevented them meeting there, and the police ordered them to leave, clearly to save them from injury and defeat. They did leave, and then the police fought our people for five hours. The police have consistently supported the fascists against the anti-fascists, but our numbers won in the end. Thank goodness!

Fighting fit: A memoir

Our organisation held a stall in Brick Lane in east London on Sundays. The fascists sold their paper nearby at the same time. One Sunday people came up to tell me, 'They're calling for Chanie Rosenberg', which meant they wanted to find and attack me. They were usually calling for Tony Cliff, my husband, our most well known leader, calling him by his real (Jewish) name Ygael Gluckstein. I was the connection to him. I was careful to stay with my comrades. But when we started going home I recognised on the other side of the road one of the fascists, who was crossing over. I didn't know whether he recognised me or not, but my reaction was immediate. As we were passing one another I put my hand to his head and pulled his hair – so hard that some of it came away. On the principle that attack is the best form of defence I subsequently used this method more than once. They were usually so surprised that they did nothing. Fortunately!

More recently the EDL (English Defence League), a fascist-friendly organisation which the fascist British National Party has members in, tried to gain political ascendancy by demonstrating *en masse* in different towns. They prepared extensively to have a national demonstration in London in 2011, on a route through Tower Hamlets in the East End which included London's main mosque which they would have attempted to demolish. We protesters, led by Unite Against Fascism, which succeeded the previous Anti Nazi League, organised against them. The result was that we had nearly 6,000 people along their route near the border of Tower Hamlets and the City of London, while they gathered 600 and did not dare to march along their intended route in Tower Hamlets. They attempted to have a rally in Sainsbury's car park, but Sainsbury's refused to allow it. They then decided to meet in two pubs in Euston. The pubs did not allow them. So they decided to travel to Tower Hamlets from King's Cross station by tube – the tube workers stopped working to prevent this. So they held a brief rally in the street outside Liverpool Street tube station. This was a tremendous victory for the anti-fascists.

Seated
woman
sculpture
Chanie

Part 4
My Life

Looking back it becomes clear that my life was very full. I reckon to have had five full-time jobs (sometimes all at once):

— wife of Cliff and his book editor (in the days before computers I translated, edited and typed all of Cliff's books, which took hours and hours. I even wrote a couple of chapters in his biography of *Trotsky*, and his own autobiography, *A World to Win*);

— mother of four children, certainly a full-time job;

— full-time teacher;

— full-time union branch secretary with no facility time;

— cook, household manager and odd job performer.

Cliff was fully immersed in his book writing and political work which took up all – or more than all – of his time, so I didn't feel put upon in taking these roles. It was not a matter of seeking formal equality, but of distributing the work in the way that was most effective. And when I was at work Cliff took care of the children at home.

My niece Tamar was an excellent piano player who studied with Daniel Barenboim's father, who had been Daniel's teacher. She was due to play Beethoven's *Appassionata Sonata* at a big London concert, and spent hours practising in our living room where the piano was – and where Cliff was writing his biography of Lenin. I knew that music playing upset his thinking, and whenever it might come on in a film or elsewhere, he would start fidgeting and talking. I asked him, 'How can you write when Tamar practises her music?' He replied, 'That's not music. That's work!'

We had decided that our political work would prevent us from having children, but after five years of living together I found myself pregnant. Cliff still thought along the same old lines, but my attitude, once I became pregnant, changed completely and I strongly wanted to have the baby. Cliff accepted this as my right, and in due course Elana Irene was born. We chose an easy-sounding Hebrew name largely for the sake of my parents.

Cliff was still in Ireland when she was born, probably the only Palestinian Jew in Dublin. In the same boarding house there also lived probably the only Palestinian Arab in Dublin. Cliff, now a proud new father, told him I'd borne a child, and he asked, 'Boy or girl?' 'Girl,' Cliff remarked. The reply was, 'Oh well, better luck next time.'

Cliff fell madly in love with her, like so many dads with their daughters, and played with her for hours. The interesting thing is that it did not affect our political work much at all, certainly not Cliff's. We decided to have a second child, also a girl, but she proved to have developmental difficulties and died at the age of 11 months. So we went for a third, which this time was a boy, called Jonathan David (known as Donny), who was as strong and healthy as the previous child had been weak and unhealthy. Donny, who lives in Edinburgh, on growing up and joining the SWP, was of immense help politically to Cliff, and, besides writing books separately, they wrote a number of books together.

Our next child was also a boy, Danny, who we called 'little Lenin', and then came the youngest, called Anna Zoe (A to Z to show she was the last). The only one of the four not to join the SWP in adulthood is 'little Lenin'. However, his attitude to his passion – music – is not dissimilar to Cliff's political passion (which is probably why he never joined the SWP).

Cliff duly fell in love with daughter Anna Zoe. Often I would see him smiling to himself, and knew that he was thinking of and enjoying the thoughts of Anna.

Bringing up the kids, of whom I am very proud, was a rewarding time in my busy life, although helping Cliff was equally rewarding but in an entirely different way. I feel I have had an exceptionally good and useful life and did the best I could living it.

There was another sense in which there was a division of labour between Cliff and myself. For reasons that should be clear above, Cliff's residency status in the UK was always shaky and this meant that not only was foreign travel virtually barred (because he lacked a current passport and might not get back in if he left), but he was not able to be heavily involved in activity on the streets. Meetings were possible, but other things were more difficult. If the SWP was an abstract talking shop or a sect then this would not have been a problem. We could all have lived in an ivory tower. But a key feature of our politics has always been an intense interplay of theory and practice. Cliff could not stand on street corners selling *Socialist Worker*, and through that find out how people reacted to certain headlines, what issues they talked about on sales and so on. He did not have a workplace or union in which to try different agitational strategies. He talked and talked with many comrades constantly, and I think my practical activities were an additional link for him, and likewise I gained a lot from his theoretical work.

Retirement

I retired at the age of 61 in 1983. I quote part of my leaving speech to the teachers:

When I was a youngster of about 17 I had a brain-storm and I became 'mad'. Everyone nodded their heads gravely and sympathetically and said, 'Don't worry. She'll grow out of it.' My parents said so; my teachers said so; my rabbi said so.

But the sane, normal South African experience made me grow 'madder'.

I went to the Middle East. The situation there didn't contribute to curing my 'madness'. In addition, I picked up a husband who was as 'mad' as me, or 'madder'.

So we came to England. My first entry into a school in the late 1940s went like this. The headmistress said kindly,

'You're new in this country. I'll tell you all about schools here: the cream go to the grammar schools, the milk go to the technical schools, and these' – waving her arm over the assembled 900 girls, and in a loud voice for all to hear, 'are the leftovers.'

I was outraged, and outrage is not helpful to cure 'madness'.

My subsequent studies of the English education system – or, for that matter, the education system in just about any country – the difference between Eton and Hackney Downs, for instance, both long established well-known boys' schools – served to confirm and prolong my 'malady'.

I know that the early prognosis was incorrect and that I never grew out of it because one of you only recently said to me, 'You're mad!' no doubt voicing the deep-seated convictions of many. So I end as I began – mad.

The staff have tolerated my 'madness' pretty well, and on the whole been very kind and friendly to one so grievously afflicted, for which I thank you.

Lastly I want to mention my dearly beloved pupil, one born to blush unseen – Charlie Christodoulou. Charlie came to this country when he was nine and a half, and he never learnt to speak an English I could understand, and the tone of his voice didn't help.

Charlie read with difficulty, wrote illegibly and spelt atrociously, and his knowledge of English is limited. I had him in the 2nd, 3rd and 5th years, and was always as polite as I could be about his unintelligibility.

One day Charlie came clutching something behind his back, and wanting to talk to me.

> *'What is it, Charlie?' I asked.*
> *'M…m…m…m.'*

Fighting fit: A memoir

'What's that, Charlie?'

'M…m…m…m.'

We didn't get very far. Eventually he thrust a crumpled piece of paper in my hand. It was a poem. I was thrilled, as I always am by any artistic manifestation of kids. I typed it up and suggested he write more, and he exploited with a stream of poems over a period of four to five months. He's had three of them published in an English-language Greek paper.

That and a few similar incidents in my teaching career have given me more pleasure than almost anything else, because I think, if Charlie can do something so unexpectedly wonderful, all these kids can. Only we need to create an environment with conditions in which they will not have to overcome almost insuperable obstacles which only an occasional Charlie now manages to do.

So I never grew out of my 'madness'. I'm only sorry not everyone is as 'mad' as me. Lots of people are regrettably only half-'mad'. If you feel you want to go the whole hog – I assure you it's exciting, interesting, absolutely revolutionary – see me afterwards.

What I most miss in retirement is the National Union of Teachers activity as I had always been very active. I now attend retired NUT teachers' meetings, but ironically there is little activity connected with it partly because of the success of an argument we had put in Rank and File Teacher – we campaigned to stop the local NUT associations being run by retired and head teachers, as most of them had been at the time. Once freed from the millstone of work I immediately started doing three things I had not been able to do before. Firstly, I started writing stories. They largely illustrate my attitude to social and family events. A number of them have been printed in various educational and political journals.

Secondly I took up sculpture. I had tried my hand at clay modelling before, but when I was working my life was so busy I could only do this if I was ill. Retirement gave me the opportunity to attend classes, and my house and garden are now full of the results. I never got far with painting though I loved looking at it and going to exhibitions, but for practising art it was always sculpture.

My crowning success was the acceptance of one of my pieces for the Royal Academy's summer exhibition in 2007. (I wish the 'Royal' bit could be removed, but that might need to wait for the revolution). It was influenced by Shona sculptors, a group of African artists from Zimbabwe – largely farmers who sculpted the hard stone on their hills. I fell in love with their work when it first came to London round about the beginning of the 21st century.

My sculpture class was taught by an English sculptor, who had spent a year with the Shona sculptors and brought some Zimbabwe spring stones back on his return to England. I bought one and found it so hard that in a week's carving I managed to move less than a centimetre all round the stone. I had previously sculpted an African head in plaster, and adopted this as my subject.

I had made the sculpture after applying to the Russian Consulate to go on holiday to Russia. They didn't seem to have room in the consulate for the queue, so we had to wait on the pavement outside. Just there was a bus shelter and in it sat an African woman. I stared at her and thought what a terrific sculpture she would make.

She saw me staring at her and I went back embarrassed to the visa queue. But I did subsequently look for other Africans who looked similar, and sometimes asked if I could photograph them. They thought I was mad, but it helped with the sculpture. Every day for about three weeks I went to Manor House tube station, near where I lived, at a busy time after work to watch black and white people's faces as they came out and see what, if any, differences there were between them – such as the prominence or otherwise of the cheekbones, the nose, the lips, and so on.

I spent a whole year hacking away at the hard stone, and then, on an impulse, while going to an exhibition at the Royal Academy, decided to enter it for the summer exhibition. Having never met anyone who had got a picture of sculpture accepted into the summer exhibition I was sure it would be rejected. A letter from the Royal Academy arrived saying there had been 8,500 entries. I was about to tear the letter up and throw it in the waste paper basket but read on and saw that it had been accepted. This is certainly my highest artistic achievement, as I do not in any way consider myself an artist.

One function of the Royal Academy exhibition is sale of the pieces, as currently art is valued in money terms. But I certainly did not want to part with it so put an impossibly high price of £10,000 on it. As I was a nobody as an artist, thankfully there was no sale, and I keep it as a precious possession decorating my living room, and have made copies of it for family and friends.

My third new activity on retirement was to learn how to swim, which I could not previously do. That is a bit astonishing as I grew up in a town by the sea. I went to a swimming pool, hung on to its sides and practised, until I could manage to swim and breathe at the same time. I now go swimming every day throughout the year, even in the cold, wet winter. That has helped me keep physically fit and means I might conceivably live to a hundred. So it is not just a matter of looking backward, but looking forward. What are the prospects?

Throughout my life Marxists have predicted the final end of capitalism because it is a system which fails. This truth has been borne out many times, from the Wall Street Crash of my youth, to the world crisis of today. The other side of the equation is the fightback. This too has been a constant feature. But so far we have not had the breakthrough that it needed. The omens, however, are good.

The international Occupy movement of tented cities has inspired thousands, possibly millions, against the evils of capitalism. Alongside this strikes are multiplying across the world. In Britain, for example, two and a half million struck on 30 November 2011, the largest strike since the General Strike in 1926. Together they could lead to what is my main objective in life, which is to witness the introduction of a socialist society, to which most of my life's activity has been devoted. The revolutions that are taking place in the Arab world, particularly Egypt, the biggest and most advanced Arab country, which had always been in the forefront of Tony Cliff's political ambitions, and in which the struggle against the oppressive bourgeois government continues unabated, are particularly inspiring. All this is something to go on living for, and so I still constantly go on demonstrations of all sorts, including those outside the Egyptian embassy against Egypt's current military government. I shall continue to do this, and if I cannot for any reason, I am ready to quit this life.

Part 5
Appendix: Malevich & revolution

Russia for centuries had a well-developed output of the visual arts, which was expressed in two directions: one the conventional Western-type well dressed portraits and family scenes, usually of royalty and the upper classes, and landscapes; the other folk art — icons, artifacts and handicrafts produced largely by peasants in the countryside. In fact St Petersburg sported the very first public gallery in Europe in 1724.

The high level of past artistic production ensured that when Russia entered its revolutionary period with the first revolution in 1905, the heightened consciousness of the revolutionary working class would inspire the artists to a flow of works of great breadth and depth. And this was indeed the case with the large number of artists who supported the revolution. Among them was Kazimir Malevich, who actually participated in the 1905 Revolution with striking workers in what was called the Battle of the Barricades at the end of the revolutionary year.

A host of avant-garde artists and poets of great stature were infused with enthusiasm for the revolution. Had they been in the West their names would be known by all interested in art: Goncharova, Larionov, the Burliuk

Appendix:

brothers, Naum Gabo, Pevsner, El Lissitsky, Tatlin, Rodchenko, Natan Altman, etc, etc; and there was the unusual phenomenon of a large number of leading women artists besides Goncharova: Alekxandra Exter, Popova, Stepanova, Udaltsova, Rosanova. Malevich was one of these avant-garde artists. The poets included Mayakovsky. Knowledge of their names, other than Mayakovsky, is limited only because they mostly stayed in Russia after the 1917 Revolution which overthrew the Tsar and put the workers in power, and failed to be largely exposed to the Western public, as were, for instance, those Russians who emigrated to live in the West after the first flush of the revolution's golden age in the middle 'twenties, like Chagall and Kandinsky.

After the 1905 Revolution and before the 1917 Revolutions the new poets and painters lived in a perpetual state of artistic and personal rebellion against the Tsar and the bourgeoisie, New schools of art and poetry flourished from about 1907 on, the most extreme embodied in Futurism, and Moscow became the international centre of revolutionary movements in art until the First World War. So much so that leading figures like Malevich and Tatlin later claimed that there was an artistic revolution which anticipated the economic and political revolution of 1917, and the conjunction of these revolutions allowed the Russian artists to envisage the task of 'creating a new world'.

Before the 1917 Revolution, Futurist poets and painters showed complete disdain for the institutions and conventions of the bourgeois society they lived in. Mayakovsky's Manifesto was called *A Slap in the Face of Public Taste*. A group called The Donkey's Tail arose

Malevich & revolution

The knifegrinder
1912-13 Oil on canvas, 79.5 x 79.5 cm
Yale University Art Gallery

Appendix:

out of an exhibition in 1912 whose main exhibit was later exposed as having been painted by a donkey's tail with a brush tied to it.

The avant-garde artists lived a crazy Bohemian life of wild orgies. They were regarded as wonderful entertainment in avant-garde cafes frequented by rich bourgeois, who were regaled with outpourings of rhymed abuse, and who often had the police in to stop fights between artist-poets and the audience.

They walked the Moscow streets provocatively in fancy dress, with flowers, algebraic or other motifs painted on cheeks, or masks, and violently coloured shirts. Mayakovsky always wore a yellow waistcoat, Malevich a red wooden spoon, the symbol of Futurism, in his lapel, David Burlitik a top hat, Larionov and Goncharova sea shells on ears, others radishes, and so on. They tried in this way to drag the established poets and painters out of the ivory towers to which art had been relegated, out into the streets, to reconcile art and society. And they emphasised their iconoclasm with rudeness and every kind of slap in the face of the establishment. They did anything to arouse a reaction from the bourgeois stupor around them, and more than anything wanted to be recognised as valid members of a society to whose forward march they could contribute.

The new work these artists produced, alongside the traditionalist bourgeois artists, was experimental, vibrant and exciting, and often magnificent. The Amazon exhibition at the Royal Academy in London in 2000, of six leading women artists up to and after the Russian revolutions, testified magnificently to this. The themes were new – peasants, workers in various

Malevich & revolution

trades, and daily activities like washing the clothes, gardening, cleaning up, and so on. The techniques were new – with quite a lot of borrowing and influence from Russia's indigenous primitive past in the form of icons (which, incidentally had a 700-year history of development, right up to the 1917 Revolution), combined with a move away from direct representational art and towards abstraction.

Kazimir Malevich was both typical and a leader in this development. He was born in Kiev, capital of Ukraine, in 1878, to Polish parents, his father an administrator in a succession of sugar refineries. He became interested in art as a teenager, and after moving to Kursk, a hundred or so miles north of Kiev towards Moscow, in 1896, he started an art group that shared a studio and held exhibitions. He moved to Moscow in 1905, hoping to extend his art education. However, he failed the entrance exam to the Moscow School of Painting, Sculpture and Architecture in 1905, 1906 and at the third attempt in 1907. That may have turned out to be a good thing, to be forced to be an auto-didact, and he started exhibiting in 1907 and continued to do so with up and coming artists such as Goncharova, Larionov and others, and went on to exhibit in the Donkey's Tail exhibition. During this time he experimented with several styles in quick succession up to and beyond the Revolution of 1917.

His early paintings are competent but not particularly remarkable.

He later, together with others, went through a uniquely Russian neo-primitivist phase. A painting of 1912, called *Chiroposidt at the Baths,* has the humble

Appendix:

subject matter of two men wrapped in large towels on either side of a small table at the public baths, one with his leg extended to have his calluses removed, the other smoking a cigarette. The style – the massive hands and feet, schematic eyes and rhythmic bodies – are characteristic of Malevich's early neo-primitivist paintings. But there is more to the picture than that, which no Russian viewer could have missed. Perhaps the best-known and most sacred image in Russian culture depicted icons of the Old Testament Trinity, in which three angels are seated around a small table in the garden of Abraham and Sarah. According to Orthodox interpretation, the angels symbolise the three persons of the Holy Trinity, and their meal ritualistically presages the incarnation of Christ in the New Testament. Malevich's parody of this holy icon was meant to shock his viewers by the deliberate, offensive coarseness of the scene – the foot on the eucharistic altar! – Absolute sacrilege to the Russian viewers. For Malevich it was intentionally shocking, but also humorous, and he more than a few times resorted to this, or more straightforward humour.

In his early career Malevich went through an impressionist phase, the effect of which was to profoundly influence him towards 'liberating the painted elements from the contours of natural phenomena and liberating my painting *psychology* from the power of an object'. He followed this philosophy throughout his life, moving closer and closer to non-objective abstraction with passionate intensity, as we shall see, till about 1919-20 – after the 1917 Revolution

In 1912-13 he composed figures made up of cone-shaped, metallic forms, called Transrational Realism, where he can be seen to be moving away from objective representation.

It is a simple move from this to Cubism, being practised at the same time, 1913-14, in Western Europe, with its fragmentation of reality and reconstruction in a different manner.

Around 1914 he moves on to a phase called 'alogism,' tinged possibly with humorous absurdity, which combines a number of seemingly unrelated objects, such as in *An Englishman in Moscow* (whose model is a famous poet friend, Alexei Khruchenykh, called 'the Englishman'). There is the model in a top hat, a fish, an orthodox church, a ladder, a red wooden spoon, a candle, a scissors, a saw, some inscriptions, etc, etc, all seemingly having no relation to one another. To those in the know, however, these objects have known hidden meanings, all related to and brought out in the character of the model, and enhancing his image and characteristics. Alogism proclaimed the right to creative freedom of expression, and the right to be absurd. (He wasn't alone. Voronsky, the great literary and artistic critic, said that to be an artist, you have to be a bit mad.) I totally agree with him.

The next, and most important, phase of his painting developed naturally after the break-up effects of cubo-Futurism, then alogism. Malevich called this Suprematism He himself said, 'In my notes on art, I almost always connect Cubism, Futurism and Suprematisrn.' He developed Suprematism into a whole profound philosophy expressed by artistic means after coming under the sway of *zaum*, a theoretical

Appendix:

An Englishman in Moscow
1914; Oil on canvas, 88 x 57 cm;
Stedelijk Museum, Amsterdam

Black Square
1920s Oil on canvas, 106 x 106 cm
The Russian Museum, St. Petersburg

Appendix:

language meaning 'beyond the mind', or 'out there', beyond this picture, out there in space, in the cosmos. 'My new painting,' he said, 'does not belong solely to the earth. Man feels a great yearning for space, an impulse to 'break free from the globe of the earth'.' (*Kazimir Malevich*, Edited by Jeanne D'Andrea, Los Angeles 1990, p167.)

Zaum was also strongly influential in literary style and production, in which Malevich also participated, in a long-standing Russian tradition of the merging of art, literature, philosophy, politics, religion and other intellectual endeavours, and he participated with a well known modern poet and musician, creating the sets and costumes for an opera called *Victory over the Sun* (1913) which was important for him to play out many of his evolving Suprematist ideas. Suprematism, first exhibited in December 1915, took the painterly, non-objective essence of works to their ultimate extreme, in productions of vigorous geometric abstraction. This was avidly taken up by many in the avant-garde of Russian painting till 1919. Malevich went the whole hog, to the ultimate of abstraction in his first exhibition of Suprematist works, with his famous *Black Square* which became his iconic symbol, and which thereafter accompanied his signature. Malevich painted several versions of this, his most emblematic work, which he later chose as the banner for his own funeral. Painted entirely freehand, without the aid of a template or ruler, it was intended as a vacant image, which would, however, carry the mark of the painter's hand in its brushwork. In fact, a close inspection clearly reveals a number of formal and surface irregularities,. Malevich always looked upon this work as an icon; in several of his exhibitions it was hung on the wall at an acute angle – as traditional religious images were hung in Russian homes – and in a corner of the room, as if to create a sacred niche. A Russian commentator describes it: 'It was a bold and dangerous step towards the position that places man before Nothing and Everything. The *Black Square* concentrates within itself eternal, universal space, transforms itself into other total formulas, and expresses *everything* within the universe. Malevich achieved this by condensing this *everything* into an absolutely impersonal, geometric form and an impenetrable black surface. In this lies the magic of the *Black Square*.

'The Suprematist works that followed *Black Square* successfully developed the idea of overcoming the terrestrial pull. Despite their expression of forms in movement, Malevich's paintings abandoned their previous logic dictated by the laws of gravity. Forms were positioned without regard to the concepts of 'above' and 'below', which allowed them to soar in a universal space of independent structures. This soaring quality was not conveyed by illusionist means: it was not depicted, it was germane to the forms themselves. In turn, these forms did not represent anything. Their meaning is in their value as primary forms.' (Ibid, p167.)

Suprematism represented 'the painting of pure form' and 'the supremacy of pure feeling', or what he called 'non-objective, sensation.' His paring down of art to its abstract essentials anticipated the Minimalist movement of the 1960s. (*The Twentieth Century Art Book*, Phaidon, London 2000, p285.)

Suprematism ended with the production of white on white squares, the abstract to end all abstracts. Space,

Minina

Appendix:

without the pull of terrestrial gravity, led Malevich to be very interested in space travel. Suprematist forms appeared to be 'beyond the mind', 'out there' in space. White became the sole representation of infinity, while the surface, coming away from its frame, could wander freely in space. *(Moscow 1900-1930,* op cit., p97.) Malevich wrote, 'My new painting does not belong to the Earth exclusively... And in fact, in man, in his consciousness, there is a striving toward space. An urge to take off from the Earth' He followed this with a prophetic vision: 'Suprematist apparatus, if one can call it that, will be one whole, without any fastenings. A bar is fused with all the elements, just like the earth's sphere, which contains life perfectly in itself, so every constructed Suprematist body will be included in a natural organisation, and form a new satellite. One only has to find the interrelationship between the earth and the moon, two bodies racing along in space. Perhaps a new Suprematist satellite equipped with all the elements can be built between them; it will travel in its orbit, creating its own new path.' *(Malevich,* Charlotte Douglas, London 1994, p26-27.)

Appropriately, Malevich was nicknamed The Commissar of Space' *(The Commissar of Space,* John Goto and Brandon Taylor, Oxford, 1998.)
The 1917 Revolutions took place at this time, which the avant-garde painters and poets wholeheartedly embraced. Hope, expectation and passionate support were unlimited. 1 think Suprematism reflects this. It was the ultimate in painting, 'the sky's the limit' - particularly appropriate to Malevich. All the young

Suprematist Painting
1915-16; Oil on canvas, 49 x 44 cm; Wilhelm Hacke Museum,
Ludwigshafen

Appendix:

artists' genius for mockery of the old bourgeois world became a tremendous excitement for building the new proletarian world. The Futurists enthusiastically embraced the revolution and the Bolsheviks, whilst almost all the old artists who remained in the Soviet Union were boycotting the government, and sabotaging it. (Commissars couldn't even get into the old ministerial buildings.)

When Lunacharsky, who headed the Commissariat of Enlightenment (called Narkompros for short), called on the whole artistic world without discrimination (except for acknowledged counter-revolutionaries) to take up offers of art commissions, it was the Futurists who were the first to eagerly come forward. Their previous outlaw status further recommended them to Narkornpros for employment under the new proletarian regime. They therefore became as if the official artistic and literary tendency.

The socialist revolution is a leap from the reign of necessity to the reign of freedom. Lenin spelt out what this meant for the artists.

In a society based on private property the artist produces goods for the market – he needs buyers. Our revolution has lifted this pressure from the artists. It has made the Soviet state their protector and patron. Every artist, and everybody who wishes to, can claim the right to create freely according to his ideal, whether it turns out to be good or not. And so you have the ferment, the experiment, the chaos. (He hated most of what was produced, but that's beside the point.) The state as patron was a tremendous stimulus to art, especially among the young.

The commitment of the revolutionary artists was

Malevich & revolution

limitless. For instance, Mayakovsky, the pre-revolutionary wild Bohemian rebel, worked almost 24 hours a day. He even slept with a log of wood for a pillow to make it easier to wake up and work.

These artists set up factory art cells, studios for workers to practise art. They set up museums of their art all over the country, reorganised art schools, put on exhibitions and did progressive research.

There was very little 'pure art' practised between 1918-1920, when propaganda for driving out the enemy in the raging civil war took first priority. Mayakovsky's famous slogan was 'Let us make the squares our palettes, the streets our brushes.' And this indeed was accomplished: streets and public places and buildings were decorated under the charge of the artists, especially for May Day and anniversaries of the October Revolution. Posters and pageants instilled the elements of Soviet justice, education in the laws of hygiene, on how to rear chickens, plant corn, breathe properly, etc, etc. The ideal of the artists as of the Communist regime was 'the whole person.'

We must remember the conditions under which all this ambitious activity was fermenting. The civil war was ruining the country. Everyone was starving and freezing. Yet despite the Government's total concentration on winning the war and abject poverty, it gave 2 million roubles for purchasing art works and setting up museums. Between 1918 and 1921, 36 museums were set up, and 26 more were projected. Works of every school were bought. Young artists were given a studio full of machinery for the creation of 'industrial' art.

Art education was transformed from elitist academies

Appendix:

to free open entry institutions, with elected professors.
Exhibitions could be entered by anyone who thought
their work appropriate -there were no juries. Art
journals sprang up like mushrooms; many also died like
mushrooms.

The artistic atmosphere was so exciting that many
leading artists who had left Russia returned soon after
the revolution. (Kandinsky, Chagall, Gabo, Pevsner
and others.)

For the first time art was given a working job, and the
artists became, as the revolutionary ones had so
desired, responsible members of society, participating
in the productive life of the country – no more 'priests
of art' but craftsmen who fulfilled a 'social command'.
They wholeheartedly applied Marx's maxim about
philosophers to artists, saying, 'Artists have merely
depicted the world; the task is to change it.'

Malevich took a full part in the exciting ferment of the
time. But while the civil war was raging he could not
find a place to live or work in Moscow, and had to live
outside the town in a small dacha without electricity or
heating, He was offered a teaching job in the art
school in Vitebsk, a town to the south of Moscow,
then directed by Mare Chagall, which offered him
both home and working conditions and materials.
Chagall resigned his position in favour of Malevich,
who renamed the school UNOVIS, an acronym for
'Advocates of the New Art'. He practically stopped
painting at this time, putting his boundless energy into
teaching, non-easel displays and writing, largely about
the theory of Suprematism. He was not a good writer,
and much of his output was so obscure as to be
impossible to understand.

Malevich & revolution

Female worker in red
1933, Oil on canvas, 71 x 60 cm

Appendix:

He also followed the movement of artists into industry, believing that, as Trotsky put it, 'Art will become the most perfect method of progressive building of life in every field.' A leading artist, Rodzenko, wrote, 'Our task consists in imparting a Communist meaning to the material labours of construction ... We shall stress the duty to achieve a synthesis of ideoological and formal elements in order to turn laboratory work into practical activity. Our ideological options are as follows: our course is based exclusively on the theory of historical materialism, influenced by the practice of the Soviet Government, we resolve to translate our experiments from the abstract into reality'. (Moscow, 1900-1930, Edited by Serge Fouchereau, London 1988, p101.) Osip Brik, a well-known art critic said, 'In the Commune everyone is a creator - not in dreams but in life. Artists ... carry out specific, socially useful tasks ... Such work gives the artist the right to place himself on the same level as other groups of workers.' (Ibid., p.98) Malevich, true to form, went the whole hog: 'Painting has ... come full circle; the very idea of the artist is a thing of the past. A true artist is an inveterate workman who constructs and arranges fresh symmetries in the creation of nature.' (Ibid p97.)

By going into industry the artists aimed to beautify life by beautifying everyday products. Thus Popova and Stepanova went into a textile factory and produced beautiful cloths, Tatlin into engineering, EI Lissitsky amd Rodchenko into printing, photography and architecture, and Malevich into a state porcelain factory making household tableware – Suprematist paintings on plates, Suprematist teapots, and so on. He also applied Suprematism to architectural models, called Arkhitectons. His designs were never built, but his pupils' designs were.

The Vitebsk school closed in 1922, and in 1923 he was appointed director of the Petrograd Museum of Artistic Culture. The idea behind these new museums was to liberate 'new art' from the traditional museum practice which ignored its very existence.

Malevich wrote:feelingly, 'New artists have been forced to spend their lives holed up in cellars and attics, be spat on by the press and society, just so that future museum staff can reap the benefits of their valuable work.' So, in an act of social and creative self determination, the new artists declared themselves 'the only people who are properly able to address issues relating to contemporary art ... and be in charge of the country's artistic education.' Thus the creative processes involved in forming a work of art, its artistic methodology, became the central reason for exhibiting it. In other words, the museum became rather a research laboratory than a museum for art conservation, or gallery. Some titles of lectures given indicates this: 'The artist's conversion from the depiction of a likeness to the reworking of pictorial elements ('abstract composition'); The concept of painting and its evolution in contemporary art; The history of contemporary pictorial systems as a sign of the evolution in the perception of space; The literary subject and pictorial contents of paintings; Surface and volumetric-spatial consciousness' Malevich was central to this development. With Stalin's grip closing in, these creative developments became suspect, and, under accusations in a Communist newspaper of the Petrograd Museum of Artistic Culture being rife with 'counterrevolutionary sermonising and artistic

Appendix:

debauchery', it was closed in 1926. (Trotsky was exiled in 1927.)

Malevich had long wanted to travel to the West as so many other Russian artists had done, but had always been too poor. In 1927 he got permission to go, and already sensing danger for his ideas and his work, he took with him about 100 of his paintings, met leading painters like Kandinsky and held exhibitions in Warsaw and Berlin. He then left the paintings in Germany and returned to Russia without them. These exhibitions were the first large-scale exposure of his work in the West, and after his death in 1935 they were bought by the Stedelift Museum in Amsterdam and the Museum of Modem Art in New York.

As Russian art closed in towards the terrible state-imposed 'socialist realism', Malevich's passion for non-objective painting came under increasing fire. A retrospective exhibition in Moscow was cut short when it moved to Kiev, and Malevich was arrested in 1930 and imprisoned for two months where he was interrogated about the ideology of modern art. 1930 was also the year Mayakovsky committed suicide.

In the last decade of his life Malevich started painting again. Partly he needed to make up for having left so many works abroad in Germany, and he needed to supply works for exhibitions. What he produced is in my mind some of his most magnificent work. But there were problems, as he was never one who would compromise on his ideas and ideals, even under fire. The non-objectivity of his Suprematist period stayed with him, but socialist realism – and his freedom – demanded representational works. So he got out of the dilemma by putting false dates on these new works, as if they were part of his oeuvre when he was famous in Russia and his work acclaimed. There may be yet another explanation – that like a number of famous Western artists like Picasso there was a partial reversion to naturalistic portraiture after the First World War, after the abstractions of the previous decades had run their course (shown in a Paris exhibition at the Royal Academy – a beautiful photographic portrait of Picasso's wife). Here are a few of these. And indeed, having painted the abstracts to end all abstracts – the *Black Square* and the *White on White Squares* – Malevich possibly felt he could take the concept no further, and so reverted to figurative painting. But in the main his paintings of this period preserve the regular geometric purity of the Suprematist period and the theories of colour and colour combinations he had evolved, but could, at a pinch, hopefully also be included under the title of Socialist Realism. And if this was not to be the case, the false dates sufficiently obscured their chronological origins to avoid censure.

Malevich contracted cancer in 1933 and begged at the highest quarters, with prestigious back-up, to be allowed to go to the West for medical attention. This was refused and he died in 1935 aged 57, thus avoiding being 'arrested and shot', as so many of his fellow artists were a year or more later, in Stalin's great frame-up purges.

To sum up: In my mind I compare what I consider to be the two giants of the 20th century: Malevich and Picasso. They were both very self-confident about their abilities and courageous in

Appendix:

using them constantly to push art forward, by experimenting with a new idea, or theory or style (for instance, Cubism), developing it to its utmost extent, and then, when they had exhausted its possibilities, moving on to a new idea, theory or style, or one which evolved from their previous efforts, and going through this process again and again, with an equal amount of enthusiasm, passion and belief, so that in their lives they embraced numerous very different styles, all of which were influential and important in the development of art on a world scale. To my mind these two Titons were the supreme definers of 20th century art.

But Malevich ;had one important circumstance missing in Picasso's life - the actuality of the Russian Revolutions of 1905 and 1917. Picasso, who was a Communist, had an intellectual's orientation to the new society, but not the reality of the revolution, and the early attempt to build it in its exciting, invigorating golden age. And this difference influenced the direction of their artistic efforts enormously. The Bolsheviks, based in the working class which numbered a mere 3 million in a vast peasant sea of 160 million, waiting for the world revolution to come to their aid, pushed every aspect of life as far as they could, to the ultimate, to the Communist ideal.

In industry there was workers' control based on the troika of elected workers; factory representative, trade union representative and Communist Party representative. In the army officers were elected by the rank and file soldiers. In living quarters there were efforts to form communal houses, in education pupils practised self-government as regards their daily concerns and were in elected committees with teachers for curriculum organisation, and with community members where schools linked up to the community. In every walk of life thinking was in the extreme, to make the socialist dream come to life as soon as possible. And so it was with art. Suprematism was the essence of painterliness taken to its extreme, every aspect – colour, form, methodology – thoroughly researched and carried out with scientific precision, the very opposite of of the material reality that existed in the country. The specific nature of the Russian Revolution was the vibrancy of these idealistic efforts up against the backwardness of the vast mass of the population, and the urgent requirement to close that huge gap, by education, electrification and mechanisation. Malevich neatly encapsulates this urgent requirement in an article on Suprematism: 'During my research I discovered that Suprematism contains the idea of a new machine, ie, a new organismic motor which does not need wheels, steam or gasoline.' (Would that this could be, and Malevich wisely adds in brackets, 'But many proofs must be provided for this'.)

The failure of the revolution in other countries, particularly the German Revolutions of 1918 and 1923, destroyed any possibility of these dreams coming to fruition, and must surely also have influenced Malevich's cessation of painting from the early to the mid-1920s, and his late productions. But the early influence of the revolutions showed aspects of the possibilities open to artists of a successful and widespread revolution, and Malevich was a courageous and indefatigable exponent of what could be.

Appendix: